D0094659

ALSO BY ANTHONY ROBBINS

Unlimited Power

Awaken the Giant Within

Notes from a Friend

Giant Steps

Unlimited Power: A Black Choice (with Joseph McClendon III)

E B O N Y
POWER THOUGHTS

Inspirational Thoughts from Outstanding African-Americans

ANTHONY ROBBINS & JOSEPH McCLENDON III

A FIRESIDE BOOK

Published by Simon & Schuster

In keeping with our commitment to create opportunities that lead to an outstanding quality of life, I am donating 10 percent of my royalties of this book to the mentoring of young African-Americans and the Young Black College Fund.

—ANTHONY J. ROBBINS

F

FIRESIDE
ROCKEFELLER CENTER
1230 AVENUE OF THE AMERICAS
NEW YORK, NY 10020

Designed by Irving Perkins Associates

Manufactured in the United States of America

2   4   6   8   10   9   7   5   3   1

Library of Congress Cataloging-in-Publication Data

Robbins, Anthony.
Ebony power thoughts : inspirational thoughts from outstanding African-Americans /
Anthony Robbins & Joseph McClendon III.
p.   cm.
1. Success—Psychological aspects—Quotations, maxims, etc.   2. Afro-Americans—
Psychology.   I. McClendon, Joseph.   II. Title.   III. Title: Power Thoughts.
BF637.S8R552   1997
158.1′089′96073—DC21   97-37090
CIP

ISBN 0-684-82437-X

ACKNOWLEDGMENTS

If there is one thing that I have learned over the years, it's that the most worthwhile things done in life are done with a team. I would like to express my deep-felt thanks to these special souls without whom this work would have forever remained stuck in the computers, ink pens, and notebooks that clutter my desk.

To my dear friend Ms. Kerri Pohn, for all of your hard work and brilliant insight. To Joseph Bossey, for your expert counsel. To Joe, Emily, and Tani Williams, for your true friendship. To Brooks Hale, Jayne Jewel, Sir Albert Saab, Joelle Burges, and the members blast, for all the laughs and adventure. To Ms. Lisa Nichole, for your love and support. To Sam the man Georges, for your timeless "Samisms." To Ms. Sonia Satra, for your loving coaching and seeing the light in me. To Ms. Lynn Rose, for your insight and your push. To Ms. Sarah Pinckney (I hope I spelled it right . . . tee-hee), for your patience. To Ms. Kerri Kennedy, for all of your help and trust in the system. And last but by all means not least, to my dear friends and partners, Tony and Becky Robbins.

—JOSEPH McCLENDON III

To Rude Ray and Nicholas

CONTENTS

INTRODUCTION

The real power behind whatever success I have now is something I found within myself—something that's in all of us. I think, a little piece of God is just waiting to be discovered.

TINA TURNER, *I, Tina*

Since the dawn of time people have been inspired by the magical words and actions of others. Hearing about the accomplishments of great individuals, how they beat the odds and how they interpreted their life's experiences, offers us an irresistible flavor of possibility and ignites our passion to continue to reach for the brass ring and *create an extraordinary quality of life.* Studying the beliefs and values of these gifted souls gives us some insight as to how to duplicate their successes in our own lives.

This book was created from our personal need to have a comprehensive collection of success quotes and inspirational anecdotes from outstanding black role models. It grew into a user-friendly conditioning *tool for continued growth and fulfillment.*

The truth is, we can learn something from everyone. The truth also is, very often, we relate more to those whom we perceive to be more like ourselves. *There is no question that the experience of being black in America is far different than that of being white, Asian, or any other race.* Out of that recognition and respect we wanted to write this book. Out of *our* personal desire to share the power of those role models and the technology we teach, we've created what we believe is a powerful tool for inspiration and positive change.

The power within the words of our great black leaders and role models is so great that it astonishes us. By indulging in the positive accomplishments of others, we can more easily envision ourselves as potential recipients of the fruits of our own forward motion.

This book is a new dimension in inspirational literature. *Ebony Power Thoughts* is an outgrowth from our original work, *Unlimited Power: A Black Choice,* which was designed to walk you through the foundation of the most advanced tools for producing an extraordinary quality of life. And our hope for you is that *Ebony Power Thoughts* will inspire you to seek our first work and its full benefits.

As in every piece of literature that we produce, *Ebony Power Thoughts* is a deliberate call to action with a doable strategy to support it. It's a reference book, a workbook, and a measuring stick for all who seek to raise the standards in their lives and produce measurable results. It is a deliberate strategy for embedding the positive attributes of these words of wisdom into our lives so we can easily call upon them for guidance and strength.

In the pages that follow you will find some of the most beautiful, inspiring, and thought-provoking words we have read. We have gathered them from books, newspaper articles, television programs, and personal interviews.

Awareness more often than not is the first step toward change for the better, and whatever we focus our attention on is what we tend to manifest in our lives. Awareness is made up of intention and attention, so by putting our attention on thoughts that are timeless, we shift our awareness. With this shift in awareness, anything is possible.

As you read these quotations, allow yourself to hear the voices of the authors in your mind. Imagine their speech inflections and picture their faces as they speak. As your awareness changes, you can see things differently. Perhaps you are able to step outside of yourself at these times, and not be so apt to become caught up in the turbulence of disempowering thoughts and emotions.

Reading these quotations daily is like planting seeds of success and happiness in the fields of all possibilities. If we nurture these seeds with intention they will blossom into the splendor of a life that you have consciously created.

There is tremendous power in innocence. The process that follows is designed to be fun and keep the child that is inside all of us alive, playful, happy, and stimulated. Curiosity and wonder are marvelous states of mind—visit them often and you will stimulate the creative genius that lives in all of us. For young children, everything is new, so they approach things with a state of wonderment. I invite you to do the same.

Seeds will grow out of the field of all possibility—and they are being planted all of the time. It's up to us what kind of seeds will be allowed in our own personal garden. Remember, if you don't decide, someone else will decide for you. Will you plant weeds or will you plant magnificent redwoods? The choice is yours.

This book can be used in many ways—as a daily meditational dip into the field of possibilities, as a resource guide, or just as an inspirational tool from the universe. No matter how you use it, please enjoy it.

While these ideas and tools are easy, please do not let their simplicity fool you. These same words and ideas have made and continue to make the great great, the strong strong, the rich rich, and the famous famous.

Laid before you are the sterling treasures of some of the most inspirational black souls of the past two centuries. Try them on like a new set of expensive driving gloves for your imagination, for you are the captain of your own starship.

MAKE YOUR FATE!

—JOSEPH MCCLENDON III

HOW TO USE
EBONY POWER THOUGHTS
Getting the Best out of the Process

"Sometimes a winner is a dreamer who just won't quit!"

MRS. EVERY JO MCCLENDON

Much like a stone cast into a placid pond, so is the first thought that we think in the morning. The stone creates ripples that affect everything in and around the pond. Since thinking is the process of asking and answering questions, the first question that we ask ourselves in the morning has a direct effect on the rest of our day and for that matter the rest of our lives. *Thinking is the process.* By asking some

19

very specific questions first thing in the morning and before we retire at night we will be programming our nervous systems to look for what is good and best for our success, happiness, and fulfillment. By deciding in advance on the best thing to ask yourself in the morning and doing it in a very specific way, you will be causing a processional effect to take place in your own mind and subsequently your life. You will be planting the seeds that will produce the results that you desire.

We are excited for you to do this. If we may, let us share with you some tips on how to get the best results. You can use *Power Thoughts* any way you wish. You can thumb through it and use it as a quote book for inspiration, or, if you are willing to use it as a system, we think that you will find it extremely effective. It will take a mere seven to ten minutes a day.

FOUR SIMPLE STEPS

STEP ONE: MORNING QUESTIONS

These are a set of questions that you will want to ask yourself in the morning. They are designed with the understanding that what we focus on in life, we tend to feel and experience. If we focus on what is wrong, then we will experience more of it. Just as focusing on what we fear makes us more fearful, focusing on what is good and possible makes us feel more centered and confident.

Undoubtedly, what controls what we focus on are the questions that we ask. That's why we will ask questions that help elicit what's great in our lives, what's exciting, what we are excited by, etc. There won't be a set of affirmations. We can say life is great all day long and our brains will still say "bull." A question makes you search for and find out what specifically is great if you want it to be great. This is really important.

Morning Questions!

- What am I most happy about in my life now? Why does that make me happy? How does that make me feel?

- What am I most excited about in my life now? Why does that make me excited? How does that make me feel?

- What am I most proud about in my life now? Why does that make me proud? How does that make me feel?

- What am I most grateful for in my life now? Why does that make me grateful? How does that make me feel?

- What am I most committed to in my life now? How does that make me feel?

- Who do I love? Who loves me?

- How will I create even more love in my life and the lives of others?

STEP TWO: READ THE DAILY QUOTE ALOUD

Read the quote aloud, and hear the person's voice as you do. Breathe in, and think about what the author really meant and what it means to you and your life. Feel their soul in yours and sense what they must have felt to say these magical words. See and hear the author speaking to you or a group of your friends and peers. Fully associate to the moment as though you are there now.

STEP THREE: ANSWER THE QUESTIONS

Ask yourself what the quote means to you and how you can apply it to your life to create positive change.

Take a moment to answer the other questions given, so you can take the answer into your own life and make things happen. Searching for the answers is the growing and conditioning process that you will prosper from. Remember, just answer the questions and move on. You do not have to ask why or justify them. As soon as you get an idea that is positive, USE IT! It is very important to let your imagination fly. Dream and experience it as though you are in it right now. Your mind can't tell the difference between what's real and what is not when it is vividly imagined. Doing this will set your system up to expect the best and leave the rest.

STEP FOUR: SHARE WITH SOMEONE ELSE

The greatest way to learn something is to learn it as though you are going to teach it to someone else. Share with someone the quote; share with someone your thoughts for the day. Sharing with another human being gives you the chance to touch someone else in a positive way and feel great in the process.

There is magic in the process. By doing it, we feel that you will discover why *Power Thoughts* is more than just a quote book, why it is a tool to help you produce actions and final rewards for your precious life.

If you've done your best, then you will have had some accomplishments along the way. Not everyone is going to get the entire picture. Not everyone is going to be the greatest salesman or the greatest basketball player. But you can still be considered one of the best, you can still be considered a success.

MICHAEL JORDAN, *I Can't Accept Not Trying*

Q: In what ways can I share my successes and good fortune with someone else?

When we finally get it that we all control our own destinies and we take responsibility for our lives, that's when we ignite our own divine drive to take action. That's when our lives change and that's when we start getting the things and situations that we desire most.

JOSEPH MCCLENDON III, *Make Your Fate*

Q: What do I desire most in my life now that I don't already possess or experience, and how excited can I get about doing what it takes to get it?

My mother never gave up on me. I messed up in school so much they were sending me home, but my mother sent me right back.

DENZEL WASHINGTON, *Essence* magazine

Q: Who are the positive role models in my life and how grateful am I for their influence?

> *Exhaust the little moment. Soon it dies*
> *And be it gash or gold it will not come*
> *Again in this identical disguise.*
>
> GWENDOLYN BROOKS,
> "Exhaust the Little Moment"

Q: What am I most excited about now?

It's not our responsibility to prove to people who we are. Our job and responsibility is to "be." What you do is proof of who you are; manifestation is realization. People have a right to think whatever they choose to think. Just because they think it does not make it right.

IYANLA VANZANT, *Acts of Faith*

Q: What can I choose to think about myself that will empower me?

We have learned that our blemishes speak of what all humanity should not do. We understand fully that our glories point to the heights of what human genius can achieve.

Nelson Mandela,
Opening of Parliament Speech
(South Africa), May 24, 1994

Q: What am I most proud of in my life?

When you're Black in White America, it's easy to stand out. To me, that's an incredible advantage— use it!

ERROL SMITH, *Thirty-seven Things Every Black Man Needs to Know*

Q: What are some of my greatest advantages in this life?

It's OK to take care of ourselves. It's OK to be good to ourselves. When we treat ourselves well, we don't expect others to take care of us. When we treat ourselves well, we are more confident, positive, and self-assured.

CARLEEN BRICE, *Walk Tall: Affirmations for People of Color*

Q: In what ways can I be even more grateful for the gifts that I see in myself?

Adversity is a profound teacher. We should rejoice and give thanks when difficulties occur, not because of the suffering itself, but because of what will come of it.

JOAN W. ANDERSON, *Where Miracles Happen*

Q: What are some of the things that I am proud of overcoming in my life?

As we are liberated from our own fear, our presence automatically liberates others.

NELSON MANDELA, inaugural speech, 1994

Q: In what ways am I a good example of what is possible for others?

Having a healthy sense of self-esteem means reexamining our current personal belief system and tossing out those beliefs and messages that produce thoughts of self-doubt.

JULIA A. BOYD, *In the Company of My Sisters: Black Women and Self-Esteem*

Q: What are some of the things that I appreciate about myself that make me self-confident?

A man must be at home somewhere before he can feel at home anywhere.

HOWARD THURMAN, *Famous Black Quotations*

Q: Where am I most comfortable and how can I have even more of that feeling in my life? How can I help others feel even more comfortable in their environments?

I guess I approached it with the end in mind. I knew exactly where I wanted to go, and I focused on getting there. As I reached those goals, they built on one another. I gained a little confidence each time I came through.

MICHAEL JORDAN, *I Can't Accept Not Trying*

Q: Where do I really want to go?

For the most part, we are good, decent, responsible people. But we're never perfect. We will always make mistakes. There is no shame in being flawed.

CARLEEN BRICE, *Walk Tall: Affirmations*
for People of Color

Q: How can I be more forgiving of myself?

Love is the most durable power in the world . . .
Love is the only force capable of transforming an
enemy into a friend.

MARTIN LUTHER KING, JR., *I Have a Dream*

Q: Whom have I not loved yet?

Yeah, life hurts like hell, but this is how I keep going. I have a sense of humor, I've got my brothers and sisters. I've got the ability to make something out of nothing. I can clap my hands and make magic.

BILL T. JONES, *Black Pearls*

Q: What will I create good for myself, my family, and friends in the future?

There are many of us brimming with hope and anticipation for the future. Yet there are too many more who have given up.

It may take daily positive thinking to convince ourselves that we, individually, are special, gifted deserving people. We can personally inspire others by exorcising our demons—our cynicism, our destructive habits—and by acknowledging the value inside our hearts and heads, and putting it to use.

ERIC V. COPAGE, *Kwanzaa*

Q: In what new ways can I best use the gifts that have been given me?

I insisted, we must try and we must succeed or our children and grandchildren will one day rightfully ask why in the face of such calamity we did not give our best efforts. What shall we tell them— and their mothers in particular—if we don't measure up?

ARTHUR ASHE, *Days of Grace*

Q: In what ways did I give my best?

Any negro, if we're honest, would have to say that in our democracy at present, that he is never, for any one second, unconscious of the fact that he is a black American. He can never be unconscious of it in any part of the United States.

PAUL ROBESON, interview on Pacific Radio,
San Francisco (March 15, 1958)

Q: What powerful identity can I hold for myself now that will excite me to be, do, and have more in my life?

How you perceive experience and how you handle it determine how your life will turn out in the long run.

BILL COSBY, *Lear's* magazine

Q: How can I see things the way they really are and what am I willing to do to then make them the way that I want them to be?

Step by step. I can't see any other way of accomplishing anything. I always had the ultimate goal of being the best, but I approached everything step by step. Confront fear and self-doubt. Fear is an illusion.

MICHAEL JORDAN, *I Can't Accept Not Trying*

Q: What fears have I already conquered in my life?

Being a role model is not based on making people change their behavior. The honest truth is that no one changes unless she wants to.

JULIA A. BOYD, *In the Company of My Sisters: Black Women and Self-Esteem*

Q: What are some of the positive changes that I look forward to making in my life?

A nation cannot teach its youths to think in terms of distraction or oppression without brutalizing and blunting the tender conscience and sense of justice of the youths of that country. More and more we must learn to think not in terms of race or color or language or religion or of political bound-

(continues)

51

(continued from previous page)

aries, but in terms of humanity. That should be considered first; and in proportion as we teach our youths of this country to love all races and nations, we are rendering the highest service which education can render.

BOOKER T. WASHINGTON, *Black Pearls*

But the real power behind whatever success I have now is something I found within myself—something that's in all of us, I think, a little piece of God just waiting to be discovered.

Sometimes you've got to let everything go—purge yourself. I did that. I had nothing but I had my freedom. My message here, and I do hope that in this book there is a message for people, is: if you are unhappy with anything—your mother, your

(continues)

(continued from previous page)

father, your husband, your wife, your job, your boss, your car—whatever is bringing you down, get rid of it. Because you'll find that when you are free your true creativity, your true self comes out.

TINA TURNER, *I, Tina*

Q: How can I be even more creative and enjoy the process?

I am still learning—how to take joy in all the people I am, how to use all my selves in the service of what I believe, how to accept when I fail and rejoice when I succeed.

AUDRE LORDE, *Black Pearls*

Q: What is one great thing that I learned yesterday?

You have to know you can win. You have to think you can win. You have to feel you can win.

SUGAR RAY LEONARD, *Black Pearls for Parents*

Q: In what ways am I certain of winning in my life right now?

I was exploring my soul, for the first time. I have always held on to the Bible, and the things that I had learned as a little girl—The Lord's Prayer, The Ten Commandments. And I prayed every night, you could believe that. But now I was really seeking a change, and I knew that it had to come from the inside out—that I had to understand myself, and accept myself, before anything else could be accomplished.

TINA TURNER, *I, Tina*

Q: What change am I seeking?

On this day I pledge neither to shy away from growth in myself, nor to require perfection in order to like myself. I will recognize through self-love that I am in a continual state of renewal and evolution.

ERIC V. COPAGE, *Black Pearls*

Q: In what ways have I loved myself lately?

I have the original vision, and I see the film in its finished form before one frame is shot. When you get people dickering with your stuff, it distorts the vision.

SPIKE LEE, *Ebony* magazine

Q: What is my vision, my passion?

A positive attitude and behavior is the passage to a meaningful relationship with others.

BARBARA KING, *Transform Your Life*

Q: How can I love and respect others even more right now?

If you have no confidence in self you are twice defeated in the race of life. With confidence you have won even before you have started.

MARCUS GARVEY, *Acts of Faith*

Q: What am I most confident about? In what ways do I exhibit confidence?

Take responsibility, not pills, for what ails you. Find out what you are doing that is not good for you and stop. . . .

Figure out what you like to do, want to do and what you are good at and do it. Struggle—I'm outta here. Do not beat up on yourself. Do not criticize yourself. Above all, do not limit yourself. Pick yourself up. Put yourself on the path and let yourself know—I'm outta here!

IYANLA VANZANT, *Acts of Faith*

Q: How can I praise myself even more for the things that I do well, even the small things?

No one can dub you with dignity. That's yours to claim.

ODETTA, *Voices of Struggle, Voices of Pride*

Q: In what ways do I claim my own dignity? How can I empower others to do and have the same for themselves?

Love being a woman. I love every oil, every cream, or every bottle of perfume, anything made for a woman. And we need that stuff. It really says something about us, and I think it's fantastic.

Although I had a bad relationship, it didn't change my feelings about men. I love men.

TINA TURNER, *I, Tina*

Q: What do I love most about who I am?

Whether positive or negative, there's always a payoff in everything we do.

CARLEEN BRICE, *Walk Tall: Affirmations for People of Color*

Q: What have I done lately that demonstrates my hunger to grow, learn, and have an even better quality of life?

What each of us must come to realize is that our intent always comes through. We cannot sugarcoat the feelings in our heart of hearts. The emotion is the energy that motivates.

IYANLA VANZANT, *Acts of Faith*

Hatred and bitterness can never cure the disease of fear, only love can do that. Hatred paralyzes life; love releases it. Hatred confuses life; love harmonizes it. Hatred darkens life; love illuminates it.

MARTIN LUTHER KING, JR., *I Have a Dream*

Q: Who do I love, and who loves me?

I'm not afraid to ask anybody anything if I don't know. Why should I be afraid? I'm trying to get somewhere. Help me, give me direction. Nothing wrong with that.

MICHAEL JORDAN, *I Can't Accept Not Trying*

Q: Who can I share my unanswered questions with?

To give names "black" and "white" to races might seem on its face, quite ludicrous. Clearly, no human beings have skin of either color. Indeed, very few come even close to those colors.

ANDREW HACKER, *Two Nations*

Q: What could be a fun and exciting way to break the mold and create more positive choices in my life and the lives of those that I love?

The amount of people that fail is directly proportionate to the amount of people that give up.

JOSEPH MCCLENDON III,
Make Your Fate

Q: What have I persevered at in the past and emerged the victor for my efforts?

> *You Got to be Houngry.*
>
> LES BROWN, *Live Your Dreams*

Q: What drives me, where does my real passion lie?

People who let events and circumstances dictate their lives are living reactively. *That means that they don't act* on *life, they only react* to *it.*

STEDMAN GRAHAM, *You Can Make It Happen*

Q: In what ways do I call the shots in my own life? What does success mean to me?

> *When a man angers you, he conquers you.*
>
> TONI MORRISON, *Quotations from African Americans*

Q: What is the best way for me to remain calm and centered under pressure?

He who is not courageous enough to take risks will accomplish nothing in life.

MUHAMMAD ALI, *Black Pearls*

Q: In what ways am I too a champion?

I'm Black, I don't feel burdened by it and I don't think it's a huge responsibility. It's part of who I am. It does not define me.

OPRAH WINFREY, *Oprah! Up Close and Down Home*

Q: What am I most proud of?

It's amazing what we can accomplish once we lose the slave mentality.

OPRAH WINFREY, *Oprah! Up Close and Down Home*

When you are young, the silliest notions seem the greatest achievements.

PEARL BAILEY, "The Raw Pearl" in *Talking Drums: An African-American Quote Collection*

Q: In what fun ways can I be more childlike today?

You are the product of the love and affection of your parents, and throughout your life you have drawn strength and hope from that love and security.

NELSON MANDELA, *Ebony* magazine

Q: When last did I show my gratefulness to those who care for me?

Instead of always looking at the past, I put myself ahead twenty years and try to look at what I need to do now in order to get there then.

DIANA ROSS, *Essence* magazine

Q: What great things do I want to create for my future?

Sometimes we get caught up in what is bad or wrong in our lives. We forget what is "good."

CARLEEN BRICE, *Walk Tall: Affirmations for People of Color*

Q: What is the greatest gift in my life right now?

Give your brain as much attention as you give your hair and you'll be a thousand times better.

EL-HAJJ MALIK EL-SHABAZZ (MALCOLM X),
The Autobiography of Malcolm X

There is absolute magic in this being called Black—splendor and purpose in every single cell. For within us are the genetics of the warrior, who steps boldly into the future, and the connection of family that binds us together with love. There is unlimited power and innate intelligence in the very soul that drives us.

JOSEPH MCCLENDON III, *Unlimited Power: A Black Choice*

Q: In what ways do I create magic in this life? In what ways have I created magic in the past?

> *"Don't Worry, Be Happy."*
>
> BOBBY MCFERRIN, song title

Q: What am I most happy about in my life now?

Why should white guys have all the fun?

REGINALD LEWIS, from the book of the same name

You have to realize that there is something special within you, a basic goodness that you must choose to manifest in every way you can—towards your family, your profession and your planet. Each of us has something good to offer.

LES BROWN, *Live Your Dreams*

Q: What great things do I have to offer?

Ignorance is no longer an adequate excuse for failure. Why? Because virtually all limitation is self-imposed. You will soon realize that you, the individual, are a minute expression of the creator of all things and as such, you have no limitations except those accepted in your own mind.

DENNIS KIMBRO, *Think and Grow Rich: A Black Choice*

As more of us learn to express the ways in which we exclude members of our community and as we learn to candidly express our own bias, we can learn to live with both feet firmly planted in a world that is whole.

LAWRENCE OTIS GRAHAM, *Member of the Club*

Q: How can I include others more on my team?

If anybody else can do it, I can do it better. I can do whatever I make up my mind to do.

BEN CARSON, *Think Big*

> *I knew I could have been lynched, manhandled, or beaten when the police came. I chose not to move. When I made that decision, I knew that I had the strength of my ancestors with me.*
>
> ROSA PARKS, *My Story*

Q: What do I stand for? In what ways do I exhibit courage under pressure?

The Power structure is not going to save us— never has and never will. We have to take things into our own hands and save ourselves.

CAMILLE COSBY, *Wisdom of the Elders*

Q: How can I take charge of my life even more now?

> *Whatever I do, I like to do with dignity and grace.*
>
> JOE WILLIAMS, *Ebony* magazine

Q: What is it I do best? How can I help others to get the best out of themselves?

If I miss something, it's because I was handling business for our future, so we can live better.

PRODEGY, *The Source* magazine

Q: What are the important things that I am doing now that will make the future brighter for myself and the ones I love?

My whole being is devoted to making my small area of existence a work of art. I am building a world.

JEAN TOOMER, *Wisdom of the Elders*

Tell them that the sacrifice was not in vain. Tell them that by habits of thrift and economy, by the way of the industrial school and college, we are coming. We are crawling up, working up, bursting up: coming through oppression, unjust discrimination and prejudice. But throughout them all, we are coming up, and with proper habits, intelligence and property, there is no power on earth that can permanently stay our progress.

BOOKER T. WASHINGTON, *Up from Slavery*

I could make millions if I led my people the wrong way, to something I know is wrong. So now I have to make a decision. To step into a billion dollars and denounce my people or step into poverty and teach them the truth.

MUHAMMAD ALI, *Black Pearls*

Q: What's one of the most important decisions that I have made in my life?

When you decide to pursue greatness, you are taking responsibility for your life. This means that you are choosing to accept the consequences of your actions and become an agent of your mental, spiritual, physical and material success.

LES BROWN, *Live Your Dreams*

Q: In what ways am I pursuing greatness?

The black community would be better served if we applied the emotion of black pride and tempered it with intellectual honesty, recognizing that while no leader is flawless, we should not tolerate messages of hate or acts of corruption or malfeasance from any leader or spokesman.

LAWRENCE OTIS GRAHAM, *Member of the Club*

Do you have the audacity to step out from the crowd and capture what life really holds for you? If so, then there is little that you cannot accomplish if you unleash your faith.

DENNIS KIMBRO, *Think and Grow Rich: A Black Choice*

I remain an optimist because I love life and most of what it has to offer.

HAKI R. MADHUBUTI, *Claiming Earth*

Q: What greatness do I have to offer others?

> *I wasn't as smart then as I am now. But who ever is?*
>
> TINA TURNER, *I, Tina*

Q: What is one of the most important lessons that I have learned in my life?

And I prayed every night, you can believe that. But now I was really seeking a change, and I knew that it had to come from the inside out—that I had to understand myself before anything else could be accomplished.

TINA TURNER, *I, Tina*

If you don't have the best of everything, make the best of everything that you have.

Overheard in a San Diego church

> *I've always been my own man, my own person. I haven't too much of anything that did not fit me. I've always tried to tailor situations to fit me.*
>
> DEXTER KING, *Ebony* magazine

Q: In what ways can I show life what it is that I really want?

> *At last at last the past is past.*
> *I've broken free and won,*
> *And now it's time to love myself*
> *and really have some fun.*
>
> JOSEPH MCCLENDON III,
> *Make Your Fate*

Q: How can I be grateful for the times that we live in now and enjoy what I have now?

> *Let's get busy!*
>
> ARSENIO HALL, opening line of his former television
> show "The Arsenio Hall Show"

Q: What am I most excited about now?

Money is the root of every mess you can think of. There are some folks who would kill you for a nickel. Those are the sorriest folks of all.

BESSIE DELANY, *The Delany Sisters' Book of Everyday Wisdom*

Q: What is the most precious thing in my life now? What is the most precious feeling in my life now?

> *When you stop a man from dreaming, he becomes a slave.*
>
> THE ARTIST FORMERLY KNOWN AS PRINCE, *Ebony* magazine

Q: How can I best foster even more desire, creativity, and imagination in myself now?

> *Check your ego at the door.*
>
> Quincy Jones, sign that he put up at the entrance
> to the "We Are the World" recording studio

Q: In what ways do I demonstrate humility in my daily life?

We must pay for our dreams or live with our night-mares.

THE REVEREND JESSE JACKSON, *Ebony* magazine

If you have the opportunity to go out there and grab for that pot of gold, why not go for it? But you have to have your own objectives.

MICHAEL JORDAN, *I Can't Accept Not Trying*

It's important for all of us to keep in mind that before the sixties, our families were intact. They were stable units that supported one another. We must have been doing something right back then, and we can do it again.

DR. GWENDOLYN GRANT, *The Best Kind of Loving*

Q: In what ways can I honor my family and the ones whom I love even more than I do now?

No person is your friend who demands your silence or denies your right to grow.

ALICE WALKER, *Voices of Struggle, Voices of Pride*

Q: Who am I most proud of and most thankful for having in my life right now?

The door cracked for, like, 16 seconds, and I streaked through. By the time they realized I was in there, they couldn't move me. The door was already closed.

WHOOPI GOLDBERG, *Ebony* magazine

Q: How can I best prepare myself to take full advantage of the very next opportunity that comes along ready to be jumped on?

No one has appointed you the chief of the black police. You have no right to judge who is black enough and who isn't.

DENISE L. STINSON, *The Black Folks Little Instruction Book*

Q: How can I look for the good in others even more in my life?

Only those who permit themselves to be are despised.

ALEX HALEY, *Roots*

Q: In what ways do I exhibit my love for others and how can I let more love into my life now?

My life has its really rough, tumble moments, but I'm luckier than most people because I get the chance to enjoy it.

WHOOPI GOLDBERG, *Ebony* magazine

Q: How can I really enjoy life more now?

There comes a point in life when you get tired of feeling, doing, and looking bad. When that time comes you move on instantly.

IYANLA VANZANT, *Acts of Faith*

Q: What do I love most about who I am?

None of us can be strong unless we have the support of the community. And unless the community is strong, it's impossible for us to be strong. No matter how big we become.

CAMILLE COSBY, *Wisdom of the Elders*

Q: How have I given thanks for those who have gone before me?

> *I can accept not winning, but I can't accept not trying.*
>
> Michael Jordan, *I Can't Accept Not Trying*

Q: What are some of the things that I have succeeded at in the past?

Culture is the sum of your experiences. What you've been through and how you express that in painting, poetry, playwriting or however. That is your culture. I think that is the other thing that unifies Black people, it is our common culture. In addition to our common oppression, we have a common culture.

OSCAR BROWN, *Wisdom of the Elders*

Q: What's one of the most important decisions that I have made in my life?

African-American men have reached a crossroads in American history, where the constant barrage of negative images forced us to prove the skeptics wrong.

MICHAEL H. COTTMAN, *Million Man March*

Q: In the past, how have I shined when the odds were against me?

We [must] realize that our future lies chiefly in our own.

PAUL ROBESON, *Baltimore Afro-American*

Nothing can dim the light which shines from within.

MAYA ANGELOU, *Acts of Faith*

My dad told me way back that you can't use race. For example, there's no difference between a white snake and a black snake. They'll both bite.

THURGOOD MARSHAL, *Voices of Struggle, Voices of Pride*

Q: In what ways can I prepare myself to notice the greatness in others first? And how can I best let them know?

To want to learn, to have the capacity to learn, and not be able to learn is a tragedy.

MICHAEL JACKSON, *Jet* magazine

Q: What things do I look forward to mastering in the future?

The most worthwhile effort I have ever undertaken is responsibility for my own life. It's hard and it's worth it.

LEVAR BURTON, *Jet* magazine

Q: As I continue to take responsibility for my own life, what great new changes do I foresee in the future?

> *Getting through [school] isn't a laughing matter. If they drop out, they're going to miss out.*
>
> BILL COSBY, *Scholastic* magazine

Q: As I look back on my life now, what are some of the things that I stuck with and accomplished and I am proud of now?

> *Your parents are the most important people in your life. And who ever you are around is [how] you gonna act like.*
>
> MICHAEL JORDAN, *I Can't Accept Not Trying*

Q: How can I best prepare myself to take full advantage of the very next opportunity that comes along ready to be jumped on?

Being your own man does not mean taking advantage of anyone else.

FLIP WILSON, Acts of Faith

People see God every day; they just don't recognize him.

PEARL BAILEY, *Acts of Faith*

I live my life by these simple principles, these five L's of fulfillment and happiness:

LIVE your life fully.

LOVE as many and as much as possible and then some.

LAUGH hard at least three times a day; you'll live longer and be happier.

LEARN all that you can about as much as you can.

(continues)

(continued from previous page)

LIGHTEN the _____ up! Take it easy, don't be so hard on yourself and everybody else.

JOSEPH MCCLENDON III, *Make Your Fate*

Q: What am I most happy about in my life now, and how can I produce even more of it for myself and the people whom I love?

Courage may be the most important of all virtues, because without it one cannot practice any other virtue with consistency.

MAYA ANGELOU, *Black Pearls*

When I leave the ballpark, I leave everything there. When I hit the driveway, I become a husband and father.

Bo Jackson, comment during sports
news television broadcast

It is the responsibility of every adult—especially parents, educators, and religious leaders—to make sure that children hear what we have learned from the lessons of life and to hear over and over that we love them and that they are not alone.

MARIAN W. EDELMAN, *The Measure of Our Success*

Q: How can I express and demonstrate even more love to the people whom I love and the people whom I have the privilege of interacting with?

The genius of our black foremothers and forefathers was . . . to equip black folk with cultural armor to beat back the demons of hopelessness, meaninglessness, and lovelessness.

CORNEL WEST, *Famous Black Quotations*

Q: What wonderful lessons can I learn from my ancestors, and how can I apply them to my life in a positive way now?

Gray skies are just clouds passing over.

DUKE ELLINGTON, *My Soul Looks Back, 'Less I Forget*

We must use time creatively . . . and forever real-ize that the time is always ripe to do great things.

DR. MARTIN LUTHER KING, JR.,
Famous African American Quotes

Regardless of how bad things may look to us, we must weave with great faith, enthusiasm, and joy! If we do this, we will see that even the frayed and faded thread can create a most glorious tapestry.

PATRICE GAINS, *Moments of Grace*

There are two ways of exerting one's strength: one is pushing down, the other is pulling up.

BOOKER T. WASHINGTON, *Heart Full of Grace*

Love is the most durable power in the world. . . .
Love is the only force capable of transforming an
enemy into a friend.

DR. MARTIN LUTHER KING, JR.,
African American Words of Wisdom

> *Act now or forever hold your place.*
>
> JOSEPH MCCLENDON III, *Make Your Fate*

Q: What action am I most excited about taking?

When you clench your fist, no one can put anything in your hand, nor can your hand pick anything up.

ALEX HALEY, *Black Pearls*

Baby, all you have to do is stay black and die. . . .
The work is the thing, and what matters at the end
of the day is, were you sweet, were you kind, did
you get the work done?

MAYA ANGELOU, *Ebony* magazine

To many of us who attain what we may and forget those who help us along the line—we've got to remember that there are so many others to pull along the way. The further they go, the further we all go.

JACKIE ROBINSON, *Baseball Has Done It*

Most folks think that getting older means giving up, not trying anything new. Well, we don't agree with that. As long as you can see each day as a chance for something new to happen, something you never experienced before, you will stay strong.

SADIE DELANY, *The Delany Sisters'*
Book of Everyday Wisdom

Q: What new experiences and/or adventures do I look forward to doing and having in my life? How can I include others in those endeavors?

Listen and learn from people who have already been where you want to go. Benefit from their mistakes instead of repeating them. Read good books . . . because they open up new worlds of understanding.

BENJAMIN CARSON, *Gifted Hands*

> *I knew whatever I set my mind to, I could do.*
>
> WILMA RUDOLPH, *Voices of the Dream*

Q: What am I committed to doing right now?

Know whence you came. If you know whence you came, there is really no limit to where you can go.

JAMES BALDWIN, *The Fire Next Time*

Black people have no copyright on virtue. People are people: some behave badly and some don't.

RANDALL ROBINSON, *Crisis*

Grandparents somehow sprinkle a sense of stardust over grandchildren.

ALEX HALEY, *Jet* magazine

Q: What am I most thankful for in my life right now?

We are all trying to improve our lives, even if we don't make the right decisions in our attempts. Sometimes we forget that everyone is struggling with change.

PATRICE GAINS, *Moments of Grace*

Q: In what ways has change been a blessing in my life in the past? How can I look to upcoming change with a sense of even more excitement?

All music is folk music. I ain't never heard no horse sing a song.

Louis Armstrong, *New York Times* (July 7, 1971)

Q: What particular piece of music can I use to inspire and empower me?

All life is interrelated. The agony of the poor impoverishes the rich; the betterment of the poor enriches the rich. We are inevitably our brother's keeper because we are our brother's brother. Whatever affects one directly affects all indirectly.

MARTIN LUTHER KING, JR., *Where Do We Go from Here?*

We cannot stand still if we expect to grow.

LINDA M. AINA, *Sister to Sister*

Q: In what glorious ways do I anticipate growing over the next three years?

I have forgiven myself; I'll make a change. Once that forgiveness has taken place you can console yourself with the knowledge that a diamond is the result of extreme pressure. Less pressure is crystal, less than that is coal, less than that is fossilized leaves or plain dirt. Pressure can change you into something quite precious, quite wonderful, quite beautiful and extremely hard.

MAYA ANGELOU, *USA Today*

Hug your grandparents and say, "I want to thank you for what you've done to make me and my life possible."

ALEX HALEY, *Jet* magazine

Q: How can I be even more thankful and grateful of the people that helped and had a hand in raising me?

> *My friends are my heart and my ears.*
>
> MICHAEL JORDAN, *Quotations from African Americans*

Q: Who are some of the very special people in my life, and how can I show my gratitude and appreciation more to them so that they can understand how much they mean to me?

The color of the skin is in no way connected with strength of the mind or intellectual powers.

BENJAMIN BANNEKER, *Banneker's Almanac*

Indeed, he who fears actually causes his own destruction. Fear saps our energies and our ability to act in our own best interest.

CARLEEN BRICE, *Walk Tall: Affirmations for People of Color*

Q: What are some of the ways that I have stood up to and faced my fears in the past and overcome adversity?

It is important that we continue in our study, be-cause by doing so we steal a moment of stillness from the hustle and bustle of everyday life.

BARBARA KING, *Transform Your Life*

Q: What are some of the things that I look forward to mastering in the future? In what ways do I find peacefulness in my life now?

When aroused the American conscience is a powerful force for reform.

CORETTA SCOTT KING, *My Soul Looks Back, 'Less I Forget*

I must now get on with those things I've always talked about doing but put off.

HARRY BELAFONTE, *Ebony* magazine

Q: What am I most excited about finally getting done in my life?

> *History is a people's memory, and without a memory, man is demoted to the lower animals.*
>
> EL-HAJJ MALIK EL-SHABAZZ (MALCOLM X), *Talking Drums: An African-American Quote Collection*

Q: What am I most proud of right now?

Let us not try to be the best or worse of others, but let us make the effort to be the best of ourselves.

Marcus Garvey, *Marcus Garvey and Garveyism*

> *Self-deception is like a drug.*
>
> RICHARD PRYOR, *Jet* magazine

Q: What is the best, most honest thing that I can say about myself; and if I don't like it, what am I willing to do to change it?

It's time for every one of us to roll up our sleeves and put ourselves at the top of our commitment list.

MARIAN W. EDELMAN, *The Measure of Our Success*

Q: How can I appreciate the goodness that I bring to the table? What am I most thankful for about myself and my life now?

How you perceive experience and how you handle it determine how your life turns out in the long run.

BILL COSBY, *Ebony* magazine

> *Go with what got you there.*
>
> DENNIS RODMAN, *Walk on the Wild Side*

Q: What are some of my greatest talents and skills?

I wonder sometimes, "Why am I alive? What is my purpose?" And I can always find a reason.

LEALAN JONES, *Our America*

Q: What is the best part about being alive in these times?

Being a friend means mastering the art of timing. There is a time for silence. A time to let go and allow people to hurl themselves into their own history. And a time to pick up the pieces when it's all over.

GLORIA NAYLOR, *The Women of Brewster Place*

When you have not forgiven someone, the better part of your human nature is troubled by your refusal to be forgiving.

BARBARA KING, *Transform Your Life*

Q: How can I become more forgiving of myself and others?

He who is not courageous to take risks will accomplish nothing in life.

MUHAMMAD ALI, *Quotations from African Americans*

Q: What are some risks and chances that I have taken in the past and prospered as a result?

Up, you mighty race, you can accomplish what you will.

MARCUS GARVEY, *Marcus Garvey and the Vision of Africa*

> *The human race does command its own destiny and that destiny can eventually embrace the stars.*
>
> LORRAINE HANSBERRY, *Voices of the Dream*

Q: What dreams do I have for my destiny?

If people could make it in the darkness of slavery, there is no excuse for us in the light of today's alleged freedom.

MARVA COLLINS, *USA Today* (March 7, 1983)

Q: What is no longer a struggle in my life now and how can I help others through their struggles now?

The African race is a rubber ball; the harder you dash it to the ground, the higher it will rise.

African proverb, *Wisdom of the Elders*

Q: What tests have I succeeded at in the past?

Along the way of life, someone must have the sense enough and morality enough to cut off the chain of hate.

DR. MARTIN LUTHER KING, JR.,
Speech given at Hall Street Church,
Montgomery, Alabama (December 5, 1955)

Q: In what ways can I love my fellow man even more *now*?

We don't have an eternity to realize our dream, only the time we are here.

SUSAN TAYLOR, *Heart Full of Grace*

Q: How can I better use my time and talents to get the things that are important to me and the ones I love?

I feel no flattery when people speak of my voice. I'm simply grateful that I found a way to work around my impairment.

JAMES EARL JONES, *My Soul Looks Back, 'Less I Forget*

I am here because of the bridges that I crossed. Sojourner Truth was a bridge. Harriet Tubman was a bridge. Madame C. J. Walker was a bridge. Fannie Lou Hamer was a bridge.

Oprah Winfrey, *Oprah! Up Close and Down Home*

Q: How can I appreciate the ones that have sacrificed so that I may have the freedom that I enjoy today?

Excellence is not an act but a habit. The things you do the most are the things you will do best.

MARVA COLLINS, *My Soul Looks Back, 'Less I Forget*

> *"Divide and conquer" in our world must become "define and empower."*
>
> AUDRE LORDE, *Voices of Struggle, Voices of Pride*

Q: What am I most empowered to do right now and how do I precisely define my outcome?

America is me. It gave me the only life I know so I must share in its survival.

GORDON PARKS, *Heart Full of Grace*

Q: What great things have not happened yet in my life that I can get excited to look forward to?

My greatest desire will always be to see my people happier in this country.

JOSEPHINE BAKER, *Voices of the Dream*

Q: What are some of the things that I am proud of and happy about in my life?

If people could make me angry they could control me. Why should I give someone else such power over my life?

BENJAMIN CARSON, *Gifted Hands*

You must be willing to suffer the anger of the opponent, and yet not return the anger. No matter how emotional the opponents are, you must remain calm.

DR. MARTIN LUTHER KING, JR., *Heart Full of Grace*

Excellence is the best deterrent to racism or sexism.

OPRAH WINFREY, *Oprah! Up Close and Down Home*

A man has to act like a brother before you can call him a brother.

EL-HAJJ MALIK EL-SHABAZZ (MALCOLM X),
Heart Full of Grace

Q: In what ways have I shown my friendship to the people closest to me lately?

Yeah, life hurts like hell, but this is how I keep going. I have a sense of humor, I've got my brothers and sisters. I've got the ability to make something out of nothing. I can clap my hands and make magic.

BILL T. JONES, *Black Pearls*

When he has conquered fear, a new dimension is added to his personality. He has lived this period. He has experienced the terror and the exultation. At the root of his being, he has experienced deep ecstasy. He is a human volcano.

PEARL PRIMUS, *My Soul Looks Back, 'Less I Forget*

200

People don't pay much attention to you when you are second best, I wanted to see what it felt like to be number One.

FLORENCE GRIFFITH JOYNER, *Heart Full of Grace*

Q: How can I demonstrate my greatness even more and enjoy the process?

You tend to be afraid when someone seems foreign to you. But if you aren't careful, that can lead to bigotry.

JASMINE GUY, *Essence* magazine

Q: How can I notice more of what is great about the differences in others and look for the good list?

One isn't necessarily born with courage, but one is born with potential. Without courage, we cannot practice any other virtue with consistency.

MAYA ANGELOU, *Heart Full of Grace*

Q: In what ways have I demonstrated courage in the past and how will I demonstrate it in the future to benefit myself and the ones that I love?

My challenge to the young people is to pick up where this generation has left off, to create a world where every man, woman, and child is not limited, except by their own capabilities.

COLIN POWELL, My American Journey

Q: If I could create the perfect world, what would it be like and how would it be different?

A sure way for one to lift himself up is by helping to lift someone else.

BOOKER T. WASHINGTON, *Black Pearls*

Love in action is the answer to every problem in our lives and in this world. Love in action is the force that helped us make it to this place, and it's the truth that will set you free.

SUSAN TAYLOR, *Voices of the Dream*

Q: Who do I love and who loves me and how can I create even more love in my life and the people that I love?

Negro action can be decisive. I say that we ourselves have the power to end the terror and to win for ourselves peace and security through the land.

PAUL ROBESON, *Voices of Struggle, Voices of Pride*

Q: What powerful new decisions can I make that will make a measurable difference in my life and the lives of the people whom I love?

> *Courage is one step ahead of fear.*
>
> COLMAN YOUNG, *Heart Full of Grace*

Q: What fears have I successfully overcome in the past that are no longer in my life now?

America is essentially a dream, a dream as yet unfulfilled. It is a dream of a land where men of all races, of all nationalities, and of all creeds can live together as brothers.

DR. MARTIN LUTHER KING, JR.,
"The American Dream" speech,
Lincoln University, Oxford, Pennsylvania
(June 6, 1961)

Q: How can I create more harmony for myself, the people whom I love, and others around me?

I am alive because of the blood of proud people who never scraped or begged or apologized for what they were. They lived asking only one thing of this world, to be allowed to be. And I learned through the blood of these people that Black isn't beautiful and it isn't ugly, Black is. It's not kinky hair and it's not straight hair—it just is.

GLORIA NAYLOR, *The Women of Brewster Place*

One thing you must set aside in order to fulfill your unique possibilities is conformity.

DENNIS KIMBRO, *Daily Motivations for African-American Success*

Q: What are some of the things that I have stood up for in the past because I knew it was the right thing to do?

You don't have to march in step with somebody to recognize what they're made of. There is not and should not be a "correct" African-American way of thinking. We are entitled to diversity of thought, opinion, and perspective.

GWENDOLYN KING, speech given at annual
Blacks in Government conference,
Washington, D.C. (August 1991)

Q: When was the last time that I reached out to make a new friend? Where is that friend now?

And now—Unwittingly, You've made me dream of violets and my soul's forgotten gleam.

ALICE DUNBAR NELSON,
My Soul Looks Back, 'Less I Forget

Q: What great things that I have done and accomplished in the past am I proud of now?

Whatever the reason for lack of cooperative economic spirit in the past, I believe that African-Americans are now quite actively seeking to come together as a people with a unified vision for success.

GEORGE C. FRASER, *Success Runs in Our Race*

Q: What are some of the glorious dreams that I hold in my heart for the future of my community and the world as a whole?

Find the good. It's all around you. Find it, showcase it and you'll start believing in it.

JESSE OWENS, *Blackthink*

Whatever you do, always be on the lookout for once-in-a-lifetime opportunities. We've found that they come around about every month or so.

JOSEPH MCCLENDON III, *Make Your Fate*

Q: What opportunities do I want to show up in my life and how can I better prepare for them when they do?

We have a responsibility to succeed at the highest level to which our talents and abilities will take us.

GEORGE C. FRASER, *Success Runs in Our Race*

Q: What does true success mean to me and what steps am I taking to bring it to fruition in my life?

None of us is responsible for our birth. Our responsibility is the use we make of life.

JOSHUA HENRY JONES, *By Sanction of Law*

There is in this world no such force as the force of a man determined to rise. The human soul cannot be permanently chained.

W. E. B. Du Bois, *My Soul Looks Back, 'Less I Forget*

It is better to be part of a great whole than to be whole of a small part.

FREDERICK DOUGLASS, *Famous African American Quotes*

An education opens a person's mind to the entire world. And there's nothing more important than to make sure everyone has the opportunity for an education.

MICHAEL JACKSON, *Jet* magazine

Q: In what ways do I continue to broaden my knowledge base?

Don't be afraid of failing. It's the way you learn to do things right. It doesn't matter how many times you fall down. What matters is how many times you get up. And don't wait for everybody else before you do something.

MARIAN W. EDELMAN, *The Measure of Our Success*

Q: What are some of the great lessons that I have learned from my past mistakes?

Yes, folks today have got it all wrong. They've got this idea that self-respect means "I am a great person. I am wonderful. ME, me, me." That's not self-respect; that's vanity.

BESSIE DELANY, *The Delany Sisters'*
Book of Everyday Wisdom

Q: In what ways can and do I help others to recognize their own greatness?

Education is painful and not gained with playing games or being average.

Marva Collins, *Ebony* magazine

Q: In what ways can I make sure that I have learned something new each and every day?

It's easy to be independent when you've got money. But to be independent when you haven't got a thing—that's the Lord's test.

MAHALIA JACKSON, *Heart Full of Grace*

Q: If challenges and tests in life were just God's way of preparing us for what we ask for, what glorious things have I asked for in my future?

In truth, you must take responsibility for yourself if you are going to pursue success and a better life in this world.

STEDMAN GRAHAM, *You Can Make It Happen*

Q: What does success mean to me and how do I see it showing up in my life now and in the future?

The vibrations in the name will help you be what you must be. Always be true to yourself, and your name will carry you.

KWEISI MFUME, *No Free Ride*

Q: By what name and identity do I define myself? What is the greatest thing about that identity?

Life is better than death, I believe, if only that it is less boring, and because it has fresh peaches in it.

ALICE WALKER, *Black Pearls for Parents*

Q: What are some of the greatest gifts in my life right now?

Don't let anything stop you. There will be times when you'll be disappointed, but you can't stop. Make yourself the very best that you can make of what you are. The very best.

SADIE TANNER MOSSELL ALEXANDER, *Voices of the Dream*

Q: What powerful experiences and states of mind can I call upon to instill the drive I want in the future?

While it's great to be Black and beautiful . . . it's better to be Black and beautiful and prepared.

MARTINA ARROYO, *Voices of the Dream*

Q: What great things am I preparing myself for in my future?

> *Your own need to be shines brighter than any dream or creation than you can imagine.*
>
> JAMES EARL JONES, *Words to Make My Dream Children Live*

Q: In what ways do I shine and how do I help others to shine as well?

My mother knew her polio was not a curse but a test that God gave her to triumph over, and she instilled in me a love of him that I will always have.

MICHAEL JACKSON, *Jet* magazine

Q: What was once a major challenge in my life that I now see as a blessing?

One thing is certain. Growing older is far superior than not growing older. If given the choice, I would opt for old age, even with all its drawbacks.

LYDIA LEWIS ALEXANDER, *Wearing Purple*

Q: What is the best part about being the age that I am now?

> *I made a commitment to completely cut out drinking and anything that might hamper me from getting my mind and body together. And the floodgates of goodness have opened upon me—spiritually and financially.*
>
> DENZEL WASHINGTON, *Essence* magazine

Q: What am I completely committed to doing to ensure that I am even more healthy now?

Always remember: Life is precious—make every moment count.

JOSEPH MCCLENDON III, *Make Your Fate*

Q: How many opportunities have I had to smile and express my thankfulness today?

If you want to see a positive image, it's in your house. It's standing there washing your under-wear. If you want to see a positive image, it's cooking dinner and has a job to go to in the morning.

BILL COSBY, speech given to
graduating class of Morehouse College,
February 1987

Q: In what ways do I show that I appreciate what others do who are close to me?

Anything that is as old as racism is in the bloodline of the nation. It's not any superficial thing—that attitude is in the bloodline and we have to educate it out.

NANNIE HELEN BURROUGHS, *Heart Full of Grace*

Q: In what ways can I recognize more of love and harmony in my life now?

People who are in control of their lives have that sort of focus, and because of it they are always seeking to expand their influence and grow and seek to better their lives.

STEDMAN GRAHAM, *You Can Make It Happen*

Q: What am I most focused on in my life now, and how powerful does that make me feel?

> *Make every night New Year's Eve.*
>
> DENNIS RODMAN, *Walk on the Wild Side*

Q: What excites me now? What are some of the things that I look forward to experiencing in the future?

We must trust the people. We must trust each other. . . . We must protect our own basic rights by protecting the rights of others.

FAYE WATTELTON, *Voices of the Dream*

Q: In what ways have I demonstrated trust in others and in myself?

I say that love will cure everything and people say that's oversimplifying it. It's not. It's just that love will cure everything. If I love you, I don't want you hungry because it will make me feel bad. If I love you, I don't want to fight you. If I love you, I don't want to see you raggedy. If I love you, I want you to have the best of everything. So, if I'm loving you, I'm not going to fight you because when I hit you, it hurts me.

DELLA REESE, *Wisdom of the Elders*

Instead of taking criticism as a knife to the heart or as a personal insult, you take it as an opportunity to review and improve your performance.

STEDMAN GRAHAM, *You Can Make It Happen*

Q: What are some small improvements that can I make today that will have a major positive influence on my life in the future?

Let us labor to acquire knowledge, to break down the barriers of prejudice and oppression believing that if not for us, for another generation, there is a brighter day in store.

CHARLOTTE FORTEN, *Voices of the Dream*

Education is the jewel casting brilliance into the future.

MARI EVANS, *Voices of the Dream*

Q: In what ways can I let my own imagination illuminate a path to the future that I desire?

I've been "not black enough." When I became the first black Miss America, there was feedback that I wasn't representative of black America because I didn't have true African-American features—my eyes are green, I have lighter skin.

VANESSA WILLIAMS, *USA Weekend* (June 28, 1991)

Q: In what ways am I uniquely different and how can I use those differences to be, do, and have more for myself and the ones whom I love?

> *He who controls images controls everything.*
>
> ROBERT TOWNSEND, *Voices of Struggle, Voices of Pride*

Q: If the only thing that I really have control over is my thoughts and emotions, what can I do everyday to remind myself that I determine my destiny?

Never give in, never, never, never—in nothing great or small, large or petty—never give in— except in conviction of honor and good sense.

TOM BRADLEY, *Heart Full of Grace*

Q: In what ways have I been tenacious and had faith in the past?

And one of the great liabilities of life is that all too many people find themselves living amid a great period of social change and yet they fail to develop the new attitudes, the new mental responses that the new situation demands. They end up sleeping through the revolution.

DR. MARTIN LUTHER KING, JR.,
"Remaining Awake Through a Great
Revolution" sermon, National Cathedral,
Washington, D.C. (March 31, 1968)

Q: What is the best thing about my attitude and how do I plan on making it even better?

Yes, the potential for you to feel victimized is out there, but the good news is that you can be the victor—all you have to do is develop the ability to shrug.

ERROL SMITH, *Thirty-seven Things Every Black Man Needs to Know*

Q: How can I demonstrate even more forgiveness and tolerance in the way I run my life?

It is a tremendous feeling when you stand there and watch your flag above the others. For me, it was the fulfillment of a nine-year dream, and I will never forget the country that brought me here.

JESSE OWENS, *Famous African American Quotes*

The guy who takes a chance, who walks the line between the known and unknown, who is unafraid of failure, will succeed.

GORDON PARKS, *My Soul Looks Back, 'Less I Forget*

"Sorry, we don't serve colored folks here." His reply, *"Fine, I don't eat them, just bring me a medium-rare hamburger."*

DICK GREGORY, *Heart Full of Grace*

Q: How can I bring a smile to more people's faces as I go through the day?

When one's house is on fire, should one wait for the people that set the fire to put it out?

PAUL BUTLER, *The Darden Dilemma*

Q: In what ways am I participating in my own rescue?

When I am feeling paralyzed by a task that seems too difficult, I remember that love lies at the core of my family and their legacy to me. The love gives me strength, and I can move again.

JONAH M. EDELMAN, *The Measure of Our Success*

Q: What is the easiest, quickest way to get back to the emotion of love now? And how can I experience even more of it now?

Given all of the facts cited above and according to all psychological theory, black women in America should have the highest rate of suicide, yet we press on and live on. We make up seventy percent of our congregations in our churches. We are the ones holding our homes together.

AUDREY F. BRONSON, *Sister to Sister*

Q: What are some of my greatest strengths and how will I demonstrate even more of them in the future?

I say: As long as I can stand it, God, I'll keep on keeping on. I say: When I can do a little bit more on my own, Lord, I'll do it. I say: If I have strength left in me, I'll use it. Mamma said, and I still believe her, that God helps those who help themselves. Now that's the truth.

RAY CHARLES, *Wisdom of the Elders*

Q: In what ways can I recognize the endless opportunities in this life and how can I take advantage of more of those opportunities?

Let's not spend time pining and denying blame rather than healing our divisions.

MARIAN W. EDELMAN, *The Measure of Our Success*

Q: In what areas of my life can I focus even more attention on what is working and harmonious to make it better for all those with whom I have the privilege of interacting?

> *Get in touch with your inner freak.*
>
> DENNIS RODMAN, *Walk on the Wild Side*

Q: In what ways can I be even more adventurous in my life now?

If people can learn to be racist, then they can learn to be anti-racist. If being sexist ain't genetic, then, dad gum, people can learn about gender equality.

JOHNETTA B. COLE, *Voices of Struggle, Voices of Pride*

Q: What is something that I used to do that was destructive that I no longer do?

Your ability to present yourself as a professional determines whether or not people are drawn toward you or flee from you.

GEORGE C. FRASER, *Success Runs in Our Race*

Q: In what ways do I show up as an example of what is possible?

It gives us significant advantage if we learn to benefit from the experiences of others.

BEN CARLSON, *Think Big*

Q: Who are some of the great people that I have had the privilege to learn from in the past?

People underestimate their capacity for change. There is never a right time to do a difficult thing. A leader's job is to help people have vision of their potential.

JOHN PORTER, *My Soul Looks Back, 'Less I Forget*

Our habitual patterns and unresourceful behaviors exist only as long as we do nothing to change them. Recognize them, arrest them, interrupt them, and replace them, and life will change for the better.

JOSEPH MCCLENDON III, *Make Your Fate*

Q: What am I no longer willing to stand for in my life and what am I willing to do to make sure it is no longer a part of my life and the lives of the people whom I love?

Music, dance, religion do not have artifacts as their end products, so they were saved. These nonmaterial aspects of the African-American culture were impossible to eradicate. And these are the most apparent legacies of the African past.

LeRoi Jones, *Blues People*

Q: What legacies do I wish to leave behind for others to prosper from?

Black women set family values by instilling them in the children whose parents didn't want to deal with them. These films were a big thank you to those women.

WHOOPI GOLDBERG (on playing Mammy roles in films),
Ebony magazine

Q: How can I really enjoy life more now?

The ultimate measure of a person is not where they stand in moments of comfort and convenience, but where they stand at times of challenge and controversy.

DR. MARTIN LUTHER KING, JR.,
African American Words of Wisdom

Human rights are God given, civil rights are man made.

ADAM CLAYTON POWELL, commencement speech,
Harvard University, Washington, D.C. (May 29, 1966)

Q: In what ways do I demonstrate fairness toward others? What am I most fair about in my life now?

So you want to live to be a hundred. Well, start with this one: No smoking, no drinking, no chewing. And always clean your plate.

SADIE DELANY, *The Delany Sisters'
Book of Everyday Wisdom*

Q: What are the things that I am doing right in my life that add to my health and happiness?

Fame creates its own standards. A guy who twitches his lip is just another guy with a lip twitch—unless he's Humphrey Bogart.

SAMMY DAVIS, JR., "Yes I Can" from *Talking Drums: An African-American Quote Collection*

Q: What is unique and special about my life and the way that I choose to live it?

All of us get the message, sooner or later. If you get it before it's too late or before you're too old, you'll pull through all right.

NAT KING COLE, *Ebony* magazine

Q: What are some of the greatest, most powerful lessons that I have learned in my life?

We owe our ancestors a better showing. And if we look at, and listen to, their teachings, our ancestors can show us the way.

GEORGE C. FRASER, *Success Runs in Our Race*

Q: What about my ancestors am I proud of and how can I learn more about them and how they lived?

I spent years crying in my diary. But I finally stopped finding fault with myself. We're all different, yet the same.

JASMINE GUY, *Essence* magazine

Q: How can I look for and celebrate the good in myself first and appreciate my differences?

We have been raised to never shed a tear no matter how it hurts. We can be better men if we understand that it's all right at certain moments in our life to shed a tear.

M.C. HAMMER, *Ebony* magazine

Q: In what ways can and do I show and express compassion toward others? How am I different than the generations that have gone before me?

My mother taught me that my talent for singing was as much God's work as a beautiful sunset or a storm that left snow for children to play in.

MICHAEL JACKSON, *Jet* magazine

Q: When I was much younger, what did I learn from someone who was much older that made a profound, positive difference in my life?

> *Teach the children pride. Nothing learned is worth anything if you don't know to be proud of yourself.*
>
> NANNIE HELEN BURROUGHS, *Heart Full of Grace*

Q: How can I reach out and touch a child's life with my love and kindness?

The American negro must remake his past in order to make his future.

<small>ARTHUR SCHOMBURG</small>, *Voices of Struggle, Voices of Pride*

Q: What are some of the greatest things about my past and what great meanings have I given to them?

The challenge is to become part of the struggle, to make a positive difference.

DAVID SATCHER, *Voices of Struggle, Voices of Pride*

Q: In what ways have I made a positive difference?

There is cause for almost everything.

GEORGE WASHINGTON CARVER,
Voices of Struggle, Voices of Pride

Q: What positive meaning can I give to any of the challenges in my life?

Before we even attempt to teach children, we want them to know each of them is unique and very special. We want them to like themselves, to want to achieve, and care about themselves.

MARVA COLLINS, *Working Woman* magazine

Q: What positive difference can or do I make in a child's life? How can I do even more now?

I tell you what I cherish most from the past: our family traditions, all those little rituals that bind you together. Folks today tend to be so busy and independent that they abandon the daily habits, like eating meals together, that keep you close.

BESSIE DELANY, *The Delany Sisters'
Book of Everyday Wisdom*

Q: How can I create even more to-getherness and closeness with the people whom I love?

We sometimes "jump off the temple roof" when what we really should do is sit in the quiet of the temple and meditate.

BARBARA KING, *Transform Your Life*

Q: How will I create more peacefulness and quiet in my life?

Every morning I wake up, I thank God for what I'm about to do!

DR. J, *Ebony* magazine

Q: What am I most thankful for in my life right now?

> *I say it's not the label that they put on the package, but what's in the box that counts.*
>
> ERROL SMITH, *Thirty-seven Things Every Black Man Needs to Know*

Q: What is the most powerful and satisfying way that I can think about myself, and how does it make me feel?

We count on ourselves to recognize and acknowledge our specialness. But how can we expect others to acknowledge something we neglect?

Julia A. Boyd, *In the Company of My Sisters:
Black Women and Self-Esteem*

Q: In what ways am I special and unique?

We all do "DO, RE, ME," but you have got to find the other notes for yourself.

LOUIS ARMSTRONG, *African American Wisdom*

Q: What is a song that when I think of it or hear it, it makes me feel energized and excited? In what ways do I march to the beat of a different drum?

Being a star made it possible for me to get insulted in places where the average negro could never hope to go and get insulted.

SAMMY DAVIS, JR., "Yes I Can" from *Talking Drums: An African-American Quote Collection*

Q: What are some of the things that make me laugh out loud?

> *I danced, I paid the piper and left him a big fat tip.*
>
> JOE LEWIS, *Quotations from African Americans*

Q: In what ways have I been a giver to others and how can I give more now?

Luck is when opportunity meets preparation.

DENZEL WASHINGTON, *Jet* magazine

Q: Am I prepared to greet and take full advantage of the inevitable opportunities that are just around the corner for me?

Black Power gives the African-American an entirely new dimension. It is a movement of black people, but it opens the way for all oppressed people.

KWAME NKRUMAH, from a speech called
"The Speech of Black Power"

Q: What does "black power" mean to me, and how can I use it to strengthen my will to do good for myself and others?

> *I don't really know the exact formula for success, but I do know the formula for failure: trying to please everybody.*
>
> BILL COSBY, *Scholastic* magazine

Q: In what ways am I unique and special?

Every intersection in the road of life is an opportunity to make a decision, and at some point to only listen.

DUKE ELLINGTON, *Quotations from African Americans*

Q: What are some of the great decisions that I have made in my life that I am thankful for now?

Recognition will do more to cement the friendship of races than any occurrence since the dawn of freedom.

BOOKER T. WASHINGTON,
Quotations from African Americans

Q: In what outstanding ways can I show the people that are the closest to me how much I appreciate them being in my life? How can I create more love, joy, and ecstasy for all those I have the privilege of calling my friends?

A man can't ride you unless your back is bent.

DR. MARTIN LUTHER KING, JR., sermon given
at the cathedral of St. John the Divine,
New York City (May 17, 1956)

Q: What negative pressures have I resisted in the past that I later prospered for not succumbing to?

I'll tell you something else that helps. That old saying, "Take life one day at a time," is mighty good advice. If I find myself becoming overwhelmed by it all, I focus on getting through the rest of the day, or maybe through dinner, or maybe just through the next hour.

SARAH DELANY, *On My Own at 107*

Q: What can I focus on right now that will empower me?

> *It took all that I've been through to get on the right path. You gotta believe that things will change.*
>
> THE ARTIST FORMERLY KNOWN AS PRINCE, *Ebony* magazine

Q: How can I best foster even more desire, creativity, and imagination in myself now?

We are responsible for the world in which we find ourselves, if only because we are the only sentient force which can change it.

JAMES BALDWIN, *Quotations from African Americans*

Soul is like electricity, we don't know what it is, but its force can light a room.

RAY CHARLES, *Quotations from African Americans*

Q: What are some of the things that when I think about them they cause me to become energized and excited? How can I create more magic moments in my life and in the lives of the people that I love?

Fatherhood is responsibility, it's definitely humility, a lot of love, and the friendship of a parent and child.

DENZEL WASHINGTON, *Jet* magazine

Q: What is the best thing that I pass on to my friends and family?

Make your success hinge on the successes of others and they will propel you to the top.

JOSEPH MCCLENDON III, *Make Your Fate*

Q: In what ways can I help others reach their goals faster and easier?

Don't let people put labels on you—and don't put them on yourself. Sometimes a label can kill you.

EL-HAJJ MALIK EL-SHABAZZ (MALCOLM X),
Quotations from African Americans

Q: In what positive ways can I describe myself so that I feel outstanding and powerful?

There's a child in all of us, a person who believes in a glorious future.

JASMINE GUY, *Essence* magazine

Anytime you see someone more successful than you are, they are doing something that you aren't.

EL-HAJJ MALIK EL-SHABAZZ (MALCOLM X),
Quotations from African Americans

Q: Who is somebody that I really admire for what they have accomplished and who they are?

> *Success is the result of perfection, hard work, learning from failure, loyalty, and persistence.*
>
> COLIN POWELL, *My American Journey*

Q: What or who am I the most committed and loyal to in my life now?

It's a frightening thing, and not uncommon for one person with bad intentions to corrupt others into following him.

STEDMAN GRAHAM, *You Can Make It Happen*

We've been given this position. We didn't campaign to be role models, but we accept it and try to do something with it, even though it's added pressure.

MICHAEL JORDAN, *I Can't Accept Not Trying*

Q: In what ways can I be a positive role model for others?

> *Today always comes before tomorrow.*
>
> Botswani proverb, *Acts of Faith*

Q: What can I plan today so that my tomorrows are even greater than before?

> *Man is his words.*
>
> African proverb, *Acts of Faith*

Q: What are some of the kind words that I can say to myself and others to create more value in our lives?

If you raise up the truth it is magnetic. It has a way of drawing people.

REVEREND JESSE JACKSON, *Heart Full of Grace*

Q: What great things do people say about me now?

> *I don't think black people know how to perceive me. Nor do I necessarily think people think I represent a lot of black people. Oddly enough, I'm really clear about my blackness.*
>
> WHOOPI GOLDBERG, *Ebony* magazine

Q: In what ways am I uniquely wonderful and special?

Wisdom is greater than knowledge, for wisdom includes knowledge and the due use of it.

JOSEPH SEVELLI CAPPONI, *Black Pearls*

Freed of the "victim mentality" that has been part of our collective psyche for so long, successful African-Americans are turning black into the color of opportunity.

GEORGE C. FRASER, *Success Runs in Our Race*

Q: How can I make sure that I see less color and more opportunity in this wonderful life that I have the privilege of living?

A lot of people give themselves bad advice. There are at least two people who would be multi-millionaires today if they had invested $1,000 I was asking for forty-seven years ago.

JOHN H. JOHNSON, *Succeeding Against the Odds*

Q: What is the greatest advice that I can give myself that will give me certainty right now?

You leave home to seek your fortune and when you get it, you go home to share it with your family.

ANITA BAKER, *Ebony* magazine

Q: In what ways do I and will I give back to my community and family as I attain the successes and fulfillments that I desire?

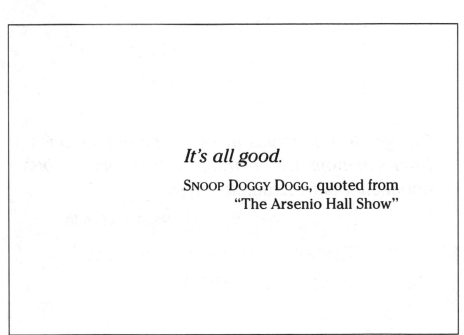

It's all good.

SNOOP DOGGY DOGG, quoted from
"The Arsenio Hall Show"

Our greatest problems in life come not so much from situations we confront as from our doubts about our ability to handle them.

SUSAN TAYLOR, *Acts of Faith*

When face to face with oneself or looking oneself in the eye, there is no copout. It is the moment of truth. I cannot lie to me.

DUKE ELLINGTON, *Black Pearls*

Q: What are some of the greatest things about who I am and what I am capable of?

I believe in human rights of everyone, and none of us is qualified to judge each other and that none of us should therefore have that authority.

EL-HAJJ MALIK EL-SHABAZZ (MALCOLM X),
Quotations from African Americans

Q: What are some great things that I can look for in others that I may not have seen before?

We must all learn to live together as brothers. Or we will all perish together as fools.

DR. MARTIN LUTHER KING, JR.,
My Soul Looks Back, 'Less I Forget

I had the knowledge and the power all the time but I did not know how to use it.

THE ARTIST FORMERLY KNOWN AS PRINCE, *Ebony* magazine

Q: In what ways can I be a positive role model for others?

Change does not roll in on wheels of inevitability, but comes through continuous struggle. And so we must strengthen our backs and work for freedom.

DR. MARTIN LUTHER KING, JR., sermon
given at the cathedral of St. John the Divine,
New York City (May 17, 1956)

Q: What positive changes do I excitedly anticipate happening in my life?

It is imperative that a woman keeps her sense of humor intact and at the ready.

> MAYA ANGELOU, *I Was Never Here and This Never Happened*

Q: When was the last time that I laughed out loud? What can I do today that will bring a smile to someone else's face?

Memories of our lives, of our works, and our deeds will continue in others.

ROSA PARKS, *Words to Make My Dream Children Live*

Q: What great things and memories will I leave behind for others to grow from?

The human animal almost never pursues power without first convincing himself that he is entitled to it.

<small>SHELBY STEELE, *The Content of Our Character*</small>

Q: Why have I decided to be, do, and have more for myself and the ones whom I love?

We want to inspire ourselves to go back to our communities and show our sons that we can do for ourselves.

ANTHONY ALLEN, *Million Man March*

Q: What great actions do I take and ways of being do I exhibit to others so that they might use me as a positive example of possibility?

Identify the things that you do well and learn to do them better.

DENISE L. STINSON, *The Black Folks Little Instruction Book*

Q: What am I outstanding in doing and what makes me so good at it? How can I help others shine even more in what they do?

> *I just want to be there in love and justice and truth and in commitment to others, so that we can make of this old world a new world.*
>
> DR. MARTIN LUTHER KING, JR.,
> "In Search of Freedom" speech

Q: How can I love even more now?

ABOUT THE ANTHONY ROBBINS COMPANIES

As an alliance of several organizations sharing the same mission, the Anthony Robbins Companies (ARC) are dedicated to constantly improving the quality of life for individuals and organizations who truly desire it. Offering cutting-edge technologies for the management of human emotion and behavior, ARC empowers individuals to recognize and *utilize* their unlimited choices.

Listed below are just some of the useful resources ARC offers you or your organization. For more information and a complete list of available services and products, please call 1-800-445-8183.

ROBBINS RESEARCH INTERNATIONAL, INC.

This research and marketing arm of the Anthony Robbins consulting and personal development business conducts public and corporate seminars worldwide. Topics range from peak performance and financial mastery to negotiating and corporate reengineering.

ANTHONY ROBBINS FOUNDATION

A nonprofit organization committed to consistently reaching and assisting individuals often forgotten by society—homeless people, the elderly, children, and the prison population—the Anthony Robbins Foundation and its volunteers provide the finest resources for inspiration, education, training, and development.

PERSONAL POWER: 30 DAYS TO SUCCESS

The *Personal Power* program is a set of twenty-four tapes that takes you through a 30-day step-by-step process for producing specific changes, mentally, emotionally, physically, and financially. The techniques and strategies are immediately applicable, and each day's action builds momentum toward a greater quality of life.

ANTHONY ROBBINS *POWERTALK!*

Each month, Anthony Robbins interviews one of the most successful men and women of our time (e.g., Norman Cousins, Sir John Templeton, Ken Blanchard). In these interviews he extracts the fundamental strategies of their achievements, whether in the areas of leadership, physical vitality and health, or financial success. With each edition of *PowerTalk!* you also receive a second audiotape in which Anthony Robbins shares his newest strategies for improving your personal and professional life. Also included is a twenty-plus-page summary of a national best-selling book so that you can keep yourself up-to-date on the newest strategies available in the marketplace today.

Robbins Research International, Inc.
9191 Towne Centre Drive
Suite 600
San Diego, CA 92122
1-800-445-8183